Joyously Triumphant's

Release the Thorns and Embrace the Rose

A guide to letting go

Marisa McClinton

Unless otherwise indicated, all Scripture quotations are taken from the Holy Bible, Scripture taken from the New King James Version®. Copyright © 1982 by Thomas Nelson, Inc. Used by permission. All rights reserved.

Published by:

Marisa McClinton

JT Consulting

New York, New York

www.Blessedbella82@gmail.com

Copyright © 2014

Marisa McClinton

A Guide To Letting Go

All rights reserved. No part of this book may be reproduced or transmitted in any form or any matter, electronic of mechanical, including photocopying, recording or by any information storage and retrieval system, without permission in writing from author/publisher/ Please direct all inquiries to blessedbella82@gmail.com.

ISBN 13-978-0692243657

Printed in the United States of America

A Guide To Letting Go

Contents

Testimony

Section I The Thorns	**15**
Chapter 1: The four elements	17
Chapter 2: How they cut	37
Section II The Rose	**48**
Chapter 3: The Solution	50
Chapter 4: Letting Go	66
The Final Word	**82**
Prayer	**86**

Dedications

Testimony

My name is Marisa McClinton and I got saved one night while sitting on the floor in a bathroom throwing up for the fourth hour straight, three months pregnant with my second child. No home, no money, and an emotionally and verbally abusive ex-boyfriend calling and harassing me every chance he got. I made the choice to leave but regretted ever meeting him in the first place. I hadn't eaten, couldn't drink, and wasn't strong enough to kill myself but I knew the pain and the exhaustion had to end. The only thing I could hear was "call Bishop". The woman I haven't spoken to in years and wasn't sure if she would even remember who I was or even care. I battled with it for a few minutes and then after throwing up for the last time, I pulled my head out of the toilet and called. I, to this day, can't remember what we talked about or how I got to the Lord's Prayer but the last thing I heard was "your saved baby". It felt like a blanket was thrown over my body. I was throwing up every hour of every day for two months and it was in that exact moment that I hung up the phone that I finally felt peace in the pit of my stomach. The tears didn't stop flowing, but the vomit sure did. For the first time in a few years I actually felt a bit of peace and serenity. I don't remember at what point I picked up that bible but there came appoint where I was so indulged in the message that no matter how many texts I received, no matter many names I was called, no matter how much money I needed, I felt in my heart that I was going to be okay. What it didn't seem like then, I can look back on it now and say that it was but a breath. Still homeless and uncertain, God placed me in a pregnancy shelter where the beginning of my life will be found. I spent the remainder of my pregnancy in this shelter, where I spent many nights learning what prayer was and discovering that that I was, was more than the mistakes I have made. The entire experience taught me that despite how many times I gave up on myself, God was there and loved me enough to give me one more chance at life, in the spiritual sense. I began to return to church and see the miracles that the kingdom designated from the altar. I began to dedicate myself and my unborn to the Lord along with the promise of making up for lost time with my eldest child. I couldn't see it then, but I look back on the series of events now and see how the kingdom set up my pain and tears for the ultimate good that I am seeing today. I have no regrets because I look back and see how I would not be where I am today without those mistakes, tears, hurts, and bad choices. This story begins on the night I got saved, but my anointed set up was prevalent far before I even knew that I was being called for service. A lifetime of mistakes and pain has led me down a road of repentance, deliverance, and yearning for healing. As I sit here on this second day of May, I examine my walk and I see how Gods hand was steadying me for this exact moment. I have been writing my entire life; in fact I have a suitcase full of marble notebooks and journals that have 30 years' worth of tears, happiness, smiles, questions, wonderment, betrayals, and threats. My entire life fits into one single suitcase etched in black and white ink. The interesting part is that I dare not to go back to those words because it's in those closets that I locked away my greatest pains, my best memories, my biggest embarrassments, and my tallest mistakes. It's not out of shamefulness but more out of closure and forward seeing. So back at the point of being in the shelter, I stood the test of time and then discovered the joy of Gods mercy. In the cusp of the shelter closing, the Lord placed me and my child in the midst of favor for the first time. From there I knew that not only was God in control of my life, but I was surrendered to his will. Over the next four years, I cannot confess that every day was peaches and sunshine. I battled many demons from within, demons sent toward my side, and demons I let right into my own house. I fought in the middle of the night with legions of spirits, gaggles of forces, and handfuls of influences. I fought spirits that dwelled within my household even before I arrived and I fought demons that I carried through my childhood that refused to let me go. I faced a period that I was required to learn how to fight on my own. I faced a desolate time where nobody could help, nobody understood, and nobody could know. In my sleep the Lord prepared me to battle; he girded me in truth and honor, he robed me in strength and fire. The Lord set my soul ablaze and then sent me forth. One night I knew that it was time to rise up. The door to hell opened and released every force that the devil had assigned to me and my path; this was it, either I was going to make it or break it. It was then that I saw myself the way that I was created. It was then that I saw through the eyes of the Lord and through the mind of the devil. It was then at 3 a.m. that was alone in complete chaos to fight against the forces of evil. I fought a fight that some Bishops won't even see in twenty five years of service. I fought a fight that at only 2 years of sanctification that many Apostles have only heard about on YouTube. It was up to me, this was it, this was the moment that I was told that I had a calling so loud on my head that the entire kingdom of hell was angry at me. God called me for such a time as this; I was Esther in the flesh and I was only a "baby Christian". I fought, and fought and fought until the sun rose. I was covered in oil and the pages of my Bible singed with the fury of hells wrath. I stood my ground and fought against forces that have never encountered a soul like mine. I had no idea what I was doing nor did I have any idea who I was. To this day, I can still smell the death of the pit in my nose, I can still feel the fire upon my face, and I can still hear the battle cries of the prayers of the Arch angels of mercy. Posted at my door, was the assigned guardsman of my father, by my side was the son of man; I wasn't expected to do anything else but to work the power that was intertwined into my DNA since the day I was conceived. No fear came over me and no harm ever came to me. From that night, I never felt the ordinary girl that I had experienced for the first half of my life. From that day I was no longer a mistake to the world, but a warrior of the kingdom. The devil had it out for me ever since that night but today I have grown into a woman of prayer, a woman of strength, and a force to be reckoned with. I have endured the pangs of suicide and have grown a heart to discern and travail the pain of the world. I've wrestled in the middle of the night with spiritual birthing pains for the delivering of the manifestation of the Lords mighty prophecy. I've heard the voice of the devil tell me to end my life; I have felt his breath on my ears as he placed the bottle of pills in my hand. I have seen his face as he poured the bags of cocaine up my nose, I have felt his hand on my throat as he poured the alcohol down my kidneys, and I have looked into his eyes as he beat the life out of me with the hands of many ex- boyfriends. I saw the devil face to face one night as I travailed in the spirit over my own soul, as the organized church didn't have the answers and nobody understood the voices that I was hearing was the voice of God instructing me towards the final fight of the seven churches.

I was given a new chance at life in 2014. The word on New Year's Eve came that the coming year was to be a year of opened doors and atmospheric shifts. In January I began to participate with a ministry that turned out to prove that God is over our every step. After being away from my family church for over a year, I was directed towards a ministry that embraced me and introduced me to God in a way that I have never known him before. The woman that I now call my God mother, was there that first day to deliver a message from God that changed my entire life and ushered me into a journey that would shift my entire purpose. In a short time I began to discover the power that God had birthed within at the day of my birth. I began to hear things and see things from the spirit realm that I only heard ministers talk about. I began to experience things that I only heard televangelists preach about. I began to know God as more than the man that worshipped on Sunday mornings, but the love of my life that I could rely on and trust with every fiber of my being. The healer that soothed my wounds and the father that corrected years' worth of self-destructive behavior. It was here that I truly found God and I allowed him into my heart.

From a mistake, to a girl, to a woman of God who has fallen short, who has cussed in the spirit, who has threatened God to take my life, who has come close to selling my soul to the devil, who has stood on the mid-Hudson bridge ready to jump to my watery death. It was then that I became the suicidal Christian; like Elijah I was lonely and depressed in the middle of my purpose. The woman who was given mighty revelation about the end times like the Apostle John, the woman who has fought the mighty warriors of hell with only the word of the king and a hand of mercy on my head. The woman of prayer who would pray for the man who beat her up and then raped her while stealing money out her purse when the rent was late. I was the woman that the kingdom made from the hurt of a lonely child hood and the fear of many abandoned relationships. I was that woman that God kept telling to keep going when she only wanted to quit. The woman who could take over thirty pills in one sitting and wake up the next day like I was just pulled from the womb. That woman, who saw her husband in her dreams and held her newborn son in her arms, the sun rose and the moon slept on my insanity. I was battered, beaten, raped, left behind, and hindered by my own fear. My insecurity ran me directly into the storm of fornication and grief. My depression walked me to the altar of unplanned pregnancy and procrastination. What took some folks a lifetime to realize, I discovered in one night with the devil. I sit here today and ask God what it means to be a woman of God, and all I hear is "look in the mirror". I hear about the church and how we behave and I mourn. I look at the members and wonder how we can pretend like God doesn't see us with our miniskirts and high school lunchroom cliques. I hear the prayers of the righteous, although they are few, and beg God to separate us by our birth right and not by our clothing or our false declaration. I sit here today and type this "testimony" and wonder how far these words will go. The last time I let the Holy Spirit type using my fingers, I told the world about how many pills I ingested the day before. Today I stand as a woman of many faces, many hats, and many reaches. Today I am a woman who just wants to be a wife, a son's mother, and Gods best earthly example. On this journey it took trust, consecration, and deep fervent prayer. Often times I wept in the parking lot of my job, many times I wanted to walk away and never look back; but my spirit never laid itself down. I had to trust God with everything that I had. It took me a few times and a few lonely nights; but I knew that I had to do it. I knew that I had to push forward and push towards the freedom that God wanted for me. It took trust for me to write my first book and submit it to the writing contest that won me a full publishing package. It took trust, the unmerited and unobvious trust in order for me to walk away from the man that wanted to marry me. It took trust and faith for me to get to the woman that I am today.

I don't want a card in my wallet letting me into the coolest church functions and backstage at the biggest concerts, I don't want a collar that lets me stand on a soap box and tell others how wrong they are, I don't want to carry just the book of God but I want to live that book; I want to be the woman at the well, the woman who's blood was dried up by just on touch. I want to be the woman who was sent to the king to risk her life for her people. I want to be the woman who led her mother in law back to her people. I want to a woman in the lion's den without a scratch, I want to be a woman in the fire without a burn, and a woman on the arc that everyone thought was crazy. Look how far God has brought me, look how long this road has been and this only talk about the past five years (give or take a few months). Look at God on my face when you see me, listen to God in my voice when I speak because this is a woman who was not meant to be breath today, a woman who was not meant to type or to think in her right mind.

2 Corinthians 5:17

New King James Version (NKJV)

¹⁷ Therefore, if anyone *is* in Christ, *he is* a new creation; old things have passed away; behold, all things have become new.

John 8:36

New King James Version (NKJV)

³⁶ Therefore if the Son makes you free, you shall be free indeed

.

Section I
The Thorns: Prick by Prick

The thorns of our existence; the spiny elements of our lives that slice our flesh and poke our spirit. It's those things that we acquire over the course of our development that prick our purpose and poke our motivation to push forward. At birth we are pure, in the womb we are untouched, but as we grow and develop into the beings that are thinking, breathing, and operating we acquire "things" that attach themselves to our character, our behavior, our speech, and our thought processes. These nouns of life affect us in ways that we sometimes do not recognize. They influence how we treat others, how we treat ourselves, how we perceive our surroundings, how we react in trouble, how we treat our relationships, how we bear our children, how we react to God, and our attitude in waiting. The nouns turn into destructive verbs which make us become the very thorns we are trying to cut off of others.

A common occurrence amongst all walks of life; there is no real distinction between race, color, creed, religious background, education, or work ethic. The thorns of life are things that we all carry around in flesh; but for some, the thorns lie dormant, ignored and untreated. The pains we suffer in our pasts become the existence we embrace in our present. We become complacent in our pain and comfortable with our thorny edges. With this section, I intend to reveal the most common thorns of our being so that we can move into embracing the roses our creation.

Chapter I

The Four Elements of Thorns: Un-forgiveness, Mistakes, Fear, Hurt

Psalm 90:8

New King James Version (NKJV)

[8] You have set our iniquities before you
our secret *sins* in the light of your countenance.

Un-forgiveness

There are instances in life that cause us pain; people let us down, families forget about us, friends leave, relationships end badly, neighbors destroy our property, bosses mistreat us, and strangers neglect us. These are the parts of life that can cut our hearts deeply and sometimes permanently. Even in times of deep hurt and deep pain, God instructs us to forgive our "neighbors" of their offenses, even our enemies who seek out to purposefully hurt, defame, and degrade us. "Easier said than done" I often rebutted when I came across that section of Gods mighty word; but there came a point when I had to reexamine the scripture for myself. I looked upon the word of God as being the ultimate instructional book for this life and the manifestations of the father; but the part I was missing was the application.

Forgiveness is spoken as being the letting go, the releasing, and the surrender of the people, places, and things of life that offend, hurt, and demoralize us. Forgiveness is said to be not for the other person, but for ourselves. That it doesn't excuse what they did, but frees our hearts to be forgiven by God and to be free from the sting of bondage; Again, easier said than done. When we hold onto unforgiveness, we open the door to resentment, bitterness, anger, frustration, depression, and defeat. When we refuse to let go of the offenses of others, we allow ourselves to relive the offense daily. I can speak to my own experiences that in my unforgiveness I often felt that by constantly reliving the offense and staying mad about it would be my revenge on that person. Although this concept made no sense, I felt within myself that I was reaping hot coals upon their heads. I was giving them their just desserts by not allowing them to forget what they did to me; in my mind. The issue with that was, they never felt a thing. They were off living their lives in their offenses to me and never had any clue or unction that I was holding on to anger; nor did they care. I was angry, but in my own mind. I was giving them the thrashing they deserved, but only in my head. I was truly living in a one man boxing arena and the only one who was feeling the punches was me. I was waking up each day and feeling what they did to me and refusing to forgive because I didn't feel that they deserved it; but the issue was, they still walked on and lived their life unaffected by what they did to me. I was making the daily choice to relive what had happened to me. Yes that's right, it was a choice I was making; I allowed myself to fall apart mentally, I allowed those offenses to reap havoc in my emotions and in my heart. I, in a sense invited it in to keep me bound and depressed. I chose to stay the victim while God was telling me that I was the victor.

I lived my days and my nights in the past. I stood on the unforgiveness that I harbored for those from my past. I allowed the manifestation of their offenses to consume me and catapult me into the hole of despair. I buckled under the pressure, I fell victim to my own self-inflicted despair. My refusal to forgive fed my emotional and mental deterioration. My spiritual health was stunted and my physical being was breaking down before my eyes.

Unforgiveness can cause the growth of the Christian to be stunted. A person cannot expand into the level of stability that God ordains if they are holding onto anger and frustration from the past. A person cannot move into the future and embrace their present if they are constantly looking backwards. The word of the Lord commands that we forgive others just as we expect our father to forgive us.

The Lord commands us to go forth and release the offenses of others and to leave the vengeance in his hands. The Lord reminds us that he is faithful to avenge our pain and to make right all of our tears; but I can honestly say, how comforting can it be when your heart just got publicly mutilated by the very wolf you allowed into your camp?

There are always those times when we are faced with the hurt and pain of heart ache, disappointment, or lack. We have such high expectations for those we trust and love and then reality sets in. the reality of the hopelessness of not receiving the love that we so gracefully gave to that undeserving person, the frustration of not receiving the apology that we feel we so gratefully deserve. The heartache and frustration of being left behind by the friends that we spent so many long nights tarrying with in prayer and supplication.

The unforgivable sins; the rape, the molestation, the murder, the abandonment, the infidelity, the cheating, the lying, the stealing, the gossiping, the backbiting, the deception, the falsehood and broken promises. Those offenses that break the human spirit into millions of pieces. Those elements that come upon us and drown out the joy that God so promised that his children were given so freely. The shallow pool of despair that is accompanied by the storm of deceit from that one-time devoted spouse and/ or lover.

It's there; those cuts, bruises, and wounds that we lick on a daily basis. "But you don't understand what they did to me!!" you yell into your pillow as God try's to console your wounded soul. We are convinced that what happened to us is the first time it's ever happened and that God has no idea how bad it hurt us. Those verbs in our lives that smack us in the face so hard that hand prints are left on our cheek. Those things that happen that make us forget that Jesus endured far worse, for far longer, and much harsher than we could ever imagine. Yes those things that knock us on the floor and pull our hair until we scream "uncle" but don't let go. Those things that make forgiveness and emotional impossibility and freedom an illusion.

"But you don't understand what they did to me!!"

These are the things that God said that we are to lay at his feet. The things that we are to surrender to him and release unto the heavens. These are the elements of our iniquities that God said will keep us from the kingdom of heaven. The seed of unforgiveness and unrighteousness is planted amongst the field of our hurts; it's up to us to make the choice to allow them to take root or to pluck them up before they choke out the ears ability to hear the unction's of the Lord.

John 20:23

New King James Version (NKJV)

[23] If you forgive the sins of any, they are forgiven them; if you retain the *sins* of any, they are retained."

Mistakes

I am an expert on holding onto personal mistakes. The greatest form of bondage that the enemy uses is to remind us of all the ways that we have failed.

Alexander Pope quoted "To err is human; to forgive is divine" We are designed to be human; not perfect. When God created us he was well informed as to how imperfectly we will stumble through this life; the only issue is, we don't realize that. We go through life and make a forest full of mistakes and failures. There are relationships that we fail to covet, education we fail to embrace, words we mistakenly let go, and bad decisions we mistakenly make.

These are elements of our lives that are given with no way of getting around. In our mistakes we learn and are supposed to press on; but with many of us, we make these mistakes and get stuck on what we have done wrong. We don't allow ourselves the freedom to embrace our humanistic state and allow God to hand over the mercy that he has so graciously promised to give.

"We are designed to be human; not perfect."

When we make the unintentional choice to hold onto our mistakes in shame, we tell God that he is unable to redeem us for the flaws we are making evident daily. Shame is from the devil; he watches and waits for us to make a mistake and then he kneads the dough of our iniquities with guilt and embarrassment, giving us the chisel that we unknowingly use to break away at our own confidence. While we are wallowing in the mistakes that we have made, the trust, security, and identity that God has given to us at birth is being surrendered for the sake of the enemy's plan to weaken us to the point of manipulation.

Think about what happens when a friend betrays you or fails to live up to the standards you have placed on them; the trust you have for them begins to dissipate and the bug of doubt begins to burrow into the far recesses of your mind. The same goes with ourselves; when we make a mistake and then another and then another, we begin to question the trust we have over our decision making skills. We begin to walk in doubt of our thinking process, and begin to question if we are truly sane or not.

I confess, I have been practicing celibacy on and off for about four years; and I say on and off because I've made many mistakes. There would always come a time when my flesh would become weak and I would falter and stumble on my baby Christian legs. Of course after each fall I would wallow in my mistake and allow the enemy to guilt me and shame me for many weeks after God has forgiven me. I know enough to repent and ask for forgivingness but in my attempt to get back up, the enemy comes to push me back on my face with the shame of being human, imperfect, immature, and selfish. He would get directly into my ear and remind me of how bad I have hurt God and how serious I have embarrassed myself. The battle against shame became unbearable until I found it easier to sit and rest in my guilt. I began to get to the point of looking in the mirror and hating what I have become, and even speaking death over myself and my imperfect existence. The enemy didn't have to do much to get me to carry on his mission of shaming me into subjection; I allowed the guilt and shame I was feeling to carry it on for him. I held the word in my heart, but wasn't strong enough to apply it.

This cycle of shame would happen with every single mistake I have ever made. I look back on many of these falls and realize that despite how hard I fell, God forgave me instantly but it was me who was choosing to hold onto the shame that was never there. God never meant for me to be shamed into submission but to walk into submission as an overcomer; a concept that was difficult to embrace in the cusp of yet another life halting failure.

Many times when we make a mistake and we are either told about it or we realize it ourselves, we become ashamed that we have acted outside the anointed being that we desire to be within our hearts. We give ourselves to the Lord and want to be perfect for him because he is perfect for us. He is always on time and always on the ball, so as his children we desire to do the same. Just like a toddler who watches her mother put on lipstick flawlessly every morning until she tries to do the same herself and finds the red lipstick everywhere but on her tiny lips.

We are Gods toddlers watching him create miracles and speaking softly and perfectly in all of his infinite wisdom on a consistent basis; and once we try to mimic our father, we say everything but the word of God in a tone everything but sweetly and to people who are anything but the ones the message was intended for. Once the realization is there that we have performed less than substantly to what we think God expects, we immediately place ourselves on punishment and cast down ourselves until we can learn to be as flawless as our fathers. The only issue is, God does not expect us to be perfect. We wallow in our mistakes and ride on the horse of our failures for the rest of our lives for no reason, simply because we have placed a higher expectation on ourselves than God ever thought to place on us. We whip and beat ourselves daily not for the sake of the father, but for the sake of pride.

In this state of dissention, we fail to realize that God is speaking forgiveness into our lives and that we are instructed to get back on our feet and move forward from the hole that we have dug ourselves. The roots of the bondages of our lives are sown from the reluctance to accept and release the mistakes bred from our humanistic existence.

"We are Gods toddlers watching him create miracles and speaking softly and perfectly in all of his infinite wisdom on a consistent basis."

Fear

Fear: False Evidence Appearing Real. The thorns in the sides of our purpose, our plans, our goals, our expansion, our faith, our walk, our friendships, our relationships, our growth, and our very beings. Fear can cripple and stagnate a person into the type of submission that can destroy a dream and create resentment and bitterness. Being afraid to walk out on faith can hold up many blessings and tools needed for spiritual growth. The fear of the unknown and uncertain can cause a person to not try anything new or experience anything life changing.

Fear is one of the greatest tools that the enemy uses to keep Gods children from stepping into the radical atmosphere that God has set aside for his remnant. We are held captive by the "what-ifs" "what – now's" and the "how will it's" the enemy knows what to say at the precise time to get us to fear walking forward into the destiny and joy that our father has promised us. We think ourselves into our spiritual deaths; we "consider" ourselves into stagnation.

Fear is such a crippling matter because it refuses to let in faith and gets hung up on the logic of a thing. God is not one to be easily understood; even Jesus questioned what God was up to at times. He is mysterious and logical at the same time; if that makes any sense. In our feeble humanistic minds, our flesh pulls and prods to understand God through logic and science but for as long as we dwell within these brains, we will never understand him the way that we would if we were sitting at his right hand. We can see a glimpse of Gods power and character in his word and the rest is left up to faith and trust. Imagine how difficult it is to trust something you don't understand.

Back in the 60's and 70's parents would often take their developmentally disabled children to state schools for care because they simply didn't understand the complexities of their behavior and/or condition. The fear of the unknown caused thousands of children to be pawned off on the state at the mercy of workers who were complete strangers to these babies.

Fear can cause us to act irrationally, illogical, and uncommon. Fear can project us into a behavior that would cause us to regress, isolate, and quit. When faced with large tasks or uncommon assignments, like the Lord often does, the spirit of fear is waiting at the waist side to speak death to our purpose with discouragement, discontent, and discomfort. When I wrote my first article to be published in the newspaper, it took me three days to send it to the editor simply because I was scared of rejection. When I wrote my first book, it took me two years to present it to the world out of fear of what the reaction would be. Fear often crippled me into bondage and pushed me deeper into darkness.

Fear is a spirit that came forth in my life and took root in everything that I did. The more I placed my trust in God, the more the spirit of fear pushed me backwards. It was a cycle of push and shove; I would gain several feet in faith and then the spiritual atmosphere became unfamiliar and unrecognizable and I unconsciously allowed fear to push me back. Once fear comes in it's like a depressant to the motivating area of our brains. All the elements that push us to go forth and to keep walking towards our goals become sudden memories and we are no longer able to visualize the manifestation that God said was on the way.

Look at Peter, he was in a boat that was being tossed to and fro. His boat mates were of no assistance with their panicked screeches of discontent and panic. Afar off was the Lord Jesus Christ walking on the very water that was tossing the boat to each side. He stood with confidence and peace and with his hand out, instructed Peter to come forth; to take the leap of faith and to trust him. Of course there was fear during such a moment as this; fear of the unknown, fear of drowning and simply a fear of being wet. But in this fear, the Lord demonstrated that his eye is still consistently on those who seek after him. His hand is steady and his peace is abundant. This parable shows that even in the greatest amounts of fear, Jesus can still sustain our faith. It took Peter a strong sense of trust to be able to overcome the fear he felt in his heart at this given moment. For a brief moment he had dominion over fear and strength in the face of adversity. Something happened to Peter that often happens to most of us; he took his eyes off of God and allowed fear to consume and stunt his breakthrough.

There were many times in my walk that I was faced with a giant and all I needed to do was keep my eyes on Christ as I stepped forward; but I opened the door to fear when I looked away from God and began to operate in my own naturalistic self.

Fear was a thorn in my purpose that stunted my growth, stopped my dreams, and halted my expansion. I was consumed by the wrong kind of fear while scraping to touch the honorable fear of the living God. I was broken and submitted to a childlike state in the fear I had of failing at something that God had already said was mine. The fear of the world choked the confidence out of me, while God was attempting to breathe his eternal life into me.

1 John 4:18

New King James Version (NKJV)

[18] There is no fear in love; but perfect love casts out fear, because fear involves torment. But he who fears has not been made perfect in love

Hurt

"What doesn't kill you make you stronger"; supposedly. The hurts and pains of our lives, the wounds that we allow to fester and decompose in our souls are elements that contribute to our death. These wounds affect us emotionally, physically, and mentally. Often times the hurtful things of our lives are the toughest to let go of because these hurtful events come with thoughts of revenge, vengance, anger, and discontent. When a person hurts us, we immediately want them to feel the way that they made us feel. We want them to swallow what they did and live with the lump in their throat like they expected us to do. Hurt, pain, sorrow, sadness, fear, weakness, and unforgiveness all tie into this one occurrence. Hurt can be an action word or a thing; both way it cripples and stunts.

Hurt is one of the main things we hold on to because we eventually find comfort in it. A life that is filled with pain will eventually become numb to it and find solace in being wounded; I was one of these people. I spent my whole life collecting a tally of all the pain and hurt I encountered and used it as a cocoon of protection. I figured that since the pain was not going to stop coming, I might as well embrace it and use it. Eventually my tears turned into emotional numbness and my fear turned into physical impossibility. So when the time came to face my wounds and allow God to heal them, I broke out into a full blown panic attack. The idea of leaving my cocoon and becoming vulnerable to the hurts of the world gave me hives. I hated the feeling of the pain I endured and by me reshaping that pain into a barrier for my heart, I was able to numb myself to its immediate effects. If I was numb then I was able to muster enough courage to get out of bed and flick the auto pilot switch. In no way shape or form was I dealing with the pain; I was just not feeling it. I pushed it down so far that I eventually forgot that it was there. I was the walking dead....until God made the choice that it was time that I be healed for his purpose. I knew what God wanted but the idea of it crippled me into fits of tears and rage. The idea of having to dig deep and to drag out he wounds of my past caused me to have several nervous breakdowns. It was terrifying an for a long time I denied it and ran from it; but I was also running stagnant in my spiritual swamp, but I didn't care as long as I didn't have to feel anything.

I clung to this pain for dear life because it was what I knew, what I was used to. The hurt and pain, the emotional blood I trekked everywhere I went, the festering smell of my decaying wounds that never left my side was actually a sort of solace for me. Believe it or not, the sting of life became better than the comforts of home. I relied on it as an excuse and as a pillow as I wallowed in my pity. If I left it behind then that meant that I would have to face myself, the world, and feel the things that happened to me instead of run away. I would have had to feel life and feel the failure on my face instead of deny it and push it away like it never happened. The death I was feeling was the death of my insides burning because of the lack of emotional care I was giving myself. I was committing spiritual suicide and to some degree, wasn't realizing it.

The hurts we hold onto are the hurts that give the enemy room to come in and wreak havoc on our thoughts and words. For instance, I have been betrayed by many female friends in the past. I held onto this pain for a good 10 – 15 years before I was able to face the root and the cause. During this time the enemy had me looking at every single female as a threat and I was reliving the betrayal over and over again in my head like it just happened the hour before. I was replaying the movie of what happened over and over simply to justify my decision to never have a female friend ever again. I kept my wounds as a defense mechanism to protect myself from allowing other females to get into my camp and cause the same pain and betrayal; even though the reality of the situation was far less than the situation I had playing in my head.

When we hold onto hurt, we are telling God that forgiveness and healing are something we are not interest in; even though they are things that are essential to the kingdom of God and the expansions of our purpose for his sake. Holding onto hurt and anguish quenches out gifting's and causes us to act in a way that is outside the word that God has spoken over us at the time of our conception. These thorns can kill a person physically, mentally, spiritually and emotionally if they are not recognized and dealt with immediately.

"The thorn of hurt will cut deep into the skin and cause the surrounding areas to become infected and therefore render the extremity useless to the person."

The festering wound of hurt will rot out the foundation of a person's existence and cause then to develop a spiritual and emotional dementia that allows the person to be unable to live effectively in the presence of God. The thorn of hurt will cut deep into the skin and cause the surrounding areas to become infected and therefore render the extremity useless to the person. The thorn of hurt is a far greater tool of death than we recognize it to be; but is one of the easiest to remove from a person's life.

The first step is simply realizing that the pain you have embraced and become used to, is a pain that is not normal for you to feel. There is no normalcy in pain or hurt; therefore the person holding onto the thorn must realize that what they are feeling is not Gods purpose for mankind and from there the person can begin to visualize the wound as being healed instead of being reopened every time a small trigger shows its face. Seeing is believing and alongside hurt, seeing yourself healed and complete is the beginning step towards the full manifestation.

2 Samuel 22:5-6

New King James Version (NKJV)

⁵ "When the waves of death surrounded me,
The floods of ungodliness made me afraid.
⁶ The sorrows of Sheol surrounded me;
The snares of death confronted me

Psalm 55:4

New King James Version (NKJV)

⁴ My heart is severely pained within me,
And the terrors of death have fallen upon me.

Chapter II

How They Cut Below the Surface: the emotional and physical affects

Emotional Wounds

Webster's describes emotions as being:

1) A state of feeling or

2) A conscious mental reaction (as anger or fear) subjectively experienced as strong feeling usually directed toward a specific object and typically accompanied by physiological and behavioral changes in the body. (websters, 2014)

Our emotions are the leading cause of our daily moods. Without the Holy Spirits lead, our feelings will affect the way we interact, speak, see, and hear everything around us. The influence of our emotions is as strong as the thoughts in our head. The emotions of grief, anger, frustration, sadness, even joy will affect the very character we display each instant. Take a second and examine your current state; ask yourself how you are feeling and look back and seek out examples of how your current mood has been displayed in your behavior towards others. It can be surprising when we look at ourselves and realize that we are in a bad mood and we have treated every person in our path horribly because of that bad mood. In contrast, those days when we are overflowing with joy and every stranger we come in contact with becomes our most trusted friend. Our emotions can dictate how we proceed to enter in to this world on a daily basis.

"The flesh has an unrighteous ability to convince itself that it is grander than it truly is."

Our emotions can often times take us out of character and out of our lanes. With negative emotions, we find ourselves jumpy, unstable, frail, and unkind; sometimes without even knowing it. Negative emotions can be caused by bitterness, resentment, the roots of pride and haughtiness, and the spirits of leviathan and Jezebel; to only name a few.

Bitterness can cause a person to strife and bicker with others even when they do not intend to. Bitterness can lead to an unteachable spirit and cause the person great anxiety and anguish for the stagnation of their souls. I suffered from bitterness from every single horrifying thing any person has said or done to me. The bitterness I encountered caused me to lash out at myself and at the world.

It is said that ridicule is the source of bitterness; often times when a person is honest with us about ourselves concerning the things that we either don't see or choose not to see, bitterness will develop for the act of bursting our bubble. The flesh has an unrighteous ability to convince itself that it is grander than it truly is. There is a self-proclaimed sense of greatness and the moment someone challenges that notion or presents it with the truth; bitterness for the message and the messenger begin to formulate. I have heard many stories of husbands and wives in counselling blame the other for the dissolution of the marriage and in that blaming game bitterness begins to grow out of the ideal that each sides' issues and shortcomings are being presented and used to enhance fault.

    The seed of bitterness doesn't need fertile ground to grow; like a dandelion, an un-kept piece of dirt can house a field of weeds in an instant. Without the ability to recognize bitterness and the desire to cast it down immediately, the field is set to take hold and over run the possibility of accepting healthy criticism. Our emotions are the gateway to these types of character assassinating manifestations. When we are upset or angry, it is that much harder to accept criticism and shift from our iniquities. When we are depressed and heavy laden, the victim mentality waits at the door and speaks life into its assignment to prevent us from looking at correction as a positive love aspect. The emotions we bare each day are the unequivocal determinants to whether or not we will grow or regress for that specified moment in time. Whenever I was happy or full of joy, I accepted life with a glow on my face. Anything anyone said to me was taken in stride and I was able to move forward towards the expansion that God had for me in that instant; but in contrast, when I was low, I was low. In my depressed state, I was unable to face my emotions and their irrationality only to succumb to the ridiculousness they spoke into my ears. My emotions held me hostage instead of me putting them under the subjection of the highest God.

"The emotional deaths of ourselves can lead to the emotional murder of others."

When our emotions are out of line, it can cause us to behave outside of the true character that God has designed for us. The emotional deaths of ourselves can lead to the emotional murder of others. There were times in my life when I was emotionally void, emotionally dead, emotionally numb; I was checked out from feeling anything. Some may say that it's better to feel nothing than to feel pain, but being emotionally void is a space that is scary and uncertain. There is no life, no light, and no understanding. The sun on my arms felt cold and the expression on my face was blank. I couldn't feel anything; nothing made me laugh and nothing made me cry. It was such a difficult place to be in when the world around you was based upon emotion and feeling.

Our emotions are able to effect the core of our being. The very thing that draws up our character can be influenced by the very emotions that help to express our character. I was under the thumb of my emotions for a good part of my life. I was in the bondage of the feelings that were meant to be underneath my foot. I was controlled by them and in turn they controlled my interactions with everything and everyone I came into contact with daily. I was a slave to the feelings and reactions of the occurrences of my life; and I didn't realize it until after I was broken by the pruning process of the Lord Jesus Christ.

Romans 6:6

New King James Version (NKJV)

⁶ knowing this that our old man was crucified with *Him,* that the body of sin might be done away with, that we should no longer be slaves of sin.

Physical Cut

Our physical beings are feeble. Although we are created in the fathers' image; (Genesis 1:27 (NKJV);So God created man in His *own* image; in the image of God He created him; male and female He created them.) due to sin we are subject to the breakdown of our flesh on a daily basis. They say that the day we are born, we begin to die; our cells and our flesh breakdown on a minimal basis in the early stages of life and accelerate as we grow in age. There are many factors that contribute to the demise of our bodies. Aside from the environmental factors of our decay; we can be blamed for the accelerated decomposition of the bodies that we must live with for a specified amount of time. I explored the aspects of our emotions and its effect on our spiritual health; now I wish to examine the physical thorns that affect our spiritual well-being.

Whenever we experience something, good or bad, our physical bodies are affected in some way. When an emotional devastation occurs, certain hormones are released and the body reacts accordingly; which is normal considering we are emotional beings, but extended amounts of time in an extremely emotional state will cause a steady decline in our health and faculties. With many emotional occurrences comes stress, overthinking, delusions, fears, elevated heart rates, shallow breathing, over eating, depressed movement, lack of sleep, and lack of attentiveness to the physical queues are bodies are designed to give us in times of distress.

Let's take into consideration, ladies, a breakup; when we are with a man and we allow our emotions to get involved, we involuntarily become slaves to the emotions that we put in. We feel emotions of joy and love so we take extra care of ourselves to impress our men. We get dressed up, we eat right, we paint our nails, we spend extra time in the shower, we exercise, and we laugh more giving us a lighter core and a gentler disposition. Now let's consider what happens when that relationship breaks up. If our emotions are wrapped up into something and that something suddenly leaves, the body goes into a withdrawal period. We begin to THINK ourselves into a frenzy and DELUSION ourselves into a depressed state. We suddenly lose the desire to pamper ourselves, the desire to exercise, maybe even the desire to eat all together. We begin to lose sleep, lose focus, and lose motivation. Our physical bodies may experience pain such as headaches and cramps, we may experience an ill feeling such as nausea and vomiting. There are times when our joints may ache and our muscles may go weak due to lack of nourishment and movement.

These physical factors can be blamed on the emotional states of our hearts. When a negative emotion is present in our lives for an extended period of time, the body begins to react to the extended release of hormones that are naturally dispelled during certain periods of grief, sadness, depression, and even anger. As we toil through the loss of a loved one, the mind is so consumed by what has left that the thought of food displeases the stomach and the body begins to store fat for nourishment due to lack of nutrients entering in. The brain controls the body; it tells the stomach when it's full and it tells the joints when it's time to pain due to injury. The brain is the control panel behind the release of the hormones that affect our moods and defense mechanisms. When we suffer from a bad mood or a heartbreaking experience, our body is designed to act accordingly; but without self-control, the body will begin to crumble underneath the weight of the emotional baggage.

A case study on how forgiveness affects the body shows that resentment and bitterness can cause the body to begin the break down process sooner than expected; "Additionally, due to increased arousal and stress levels, many who experience prolonged resentment seek to self-medicate through alcohol, drugs, tobacco or unhealthy eating patterns—which can lead to secondary health problems. Other negative health effects of anger can include headaches, digestive issues, tachycardia (rapid heartbeat), arrhythmia (irregular heartbeat) and high blood pressure. Many of these symptoms lead dependent individuals to self-medicate to eliminate stress or anxiety, often leading to drug or alcohol addiction.

The negative health effects of un-forgiveness can also have negative effects on the brain. Studies have shown that even low-level resentment and anger tend to lower cognitive function and problem-solving capacity. Mental errors tend to increase, and alternate perspectives fall out of reach, making problems more difficult to solve. Additionally, unforgiveness can lead to negative mental health effects such as anxiety disorders, depression, and shame. Un-forgiveness can also create a physiological and psychological "crash" into depression, once incidents of hyper arousal subside." (Soberplace: negative effects of unforgivness , 2009)

The emotional aspects of our character often have a physical affect to our existence. I often suffered the physical symptoms of deep depression by experiencing body aches, swollen face and eyes from uncontrollable crying and weeping, muscle weakness from lack of mobility, and exhaustion and bloating from either excessive eating or no eating at all. I often had severe health scares due to the amount of stress and fear that I embraced on a daily basis. I discovered that for as long as we hold onto these destructive weeds, our bodies will be in a perpetual cycle of breakdown and recovery; and the more the body is forced to break and heal itself, the faster it will lose its ability to recoup and recover. The body is meant to endure only so much.

In the Old Testament, many people lived well beyond 100 years old, please well beyond 300 years old. I often wondered what the secret to long lasting life was until it was revealed to me that the aspects and elements of sin cause our bodies to break down almost instantly. The sins we carry of disobedience, lack of faith and trust, embracing demonic influence through the refusal of rebuking and denial, and the sin of fornication and lusts of the mind. All of these factors can cause a person emotional pain, mental anguish, and spiritual turmoil that can ultimately lead to the physical manifestations of migraines, hypertension, stroke, female organ breakdown, and even some cancerous conditions.

The emotional parts of our existence, outside of the subjection of the Lord Jesus Christ, will cause the human body to react in a way that is outside of the design of the father's intent. Without self-control and emotional awareness our physical wellbeing suffers and we are unable to fulfill the physical purposes for the sake of the Kingdom. Our physical states are as essential to Gods purpose as our spiritual and emotional states; a body in health is useable and a body in death, is simply food for the earth.

1 Corinthians 6:19-20

New King James Version (NKJV)

[19] Or do you not know that your body is the temple of the Holy Spirit *who is* in you, whom you have from God, and you are not your own? [20] For you were bought at a price; therefore glorify God in your body and in your spirit, which are God's

Section II
The Rose: Petal by Petal

The rose is the delicate reincarnation of our deliverance. When we go to God and surrender and allow him to create in us a new creature, we are allowing him to strip us of those thorny exteriors of our hearts and minds. The deliverance process is not a pleasant one. Like a rose, the petals of our existence must be peeled bit by bit so not to damage the delicate covering of the leaf. Our hearts are covered by the highest God and as he peels away the dead skin of our sinful lives, the healthy, new covering of our being is exposed to the light so that it can grow and flourish into the sweet smelling rose that God intended us to be at the day of our birth.

The solution lies in the healing power of Christ, but also sits in the efforts we put forth and the dedication we embody towards being made whole and complete in the eyes of the Lord. Yes, God has the power to do all things without any help from us, but he will not force us to become something that we do not want to become. He allows us free will and he gives us a choice. For those who are tired and sick of being broken and cast down, God offers his help and his healing power. He gives us the opportunity to come to him and to walk in the deliverance that is the promise of salvation and eternal life. I intend to touch upon the "who", the "what", and the "why" that is required when moving towards the wholeness that is the completed rose.

Chapter III

The Consistency of the Solution: the Who, What, and Why

The "Who": The Process of Self-Examination

Self-examination is the act of looking at one self in detail and picking apart the behaviors and thoughts that cause us to react each day. Self-examination forces us to go into the recesses of our minds and face the mirrors of our souls. We are to look at ourselves and face the good, the bad, and the ugly. This is a practice of strength and discovery. When a person begins the journey of self-examination, the person should first make the realization that we have flaws and the face we will see staring back at us will be drastically different from the ideal we have orchestrated of ourselves. When self-examination is done correctly, humility and confession will become the direct result. The process towards the solution plays out like this: first, self-examination, self-admitting, confession, and then repentance.

There was a point in my journey where self-examination was essential to moving forward. My denial of who I truly was, was hindering me from facing this person and changing this person. The journey was not light by no means. It hurt, I cried, I screamed, I felt shame, and I wanted to quit several hundred times. When I looked at myself, my world came crashing down because I saw that I wasn't the grandiose stigma that I created for myself. I saw a being who was broken, afraid, lost, hurt, and incomplete.

I always had a problem with looking myself in the eye; I would always look at myself in the mirror but could never look myself in the core of my eye. One day during this process, I felt the Lord tell me that it was time to look at myself but this time I had to look into the core of my soul; I had to look myself in the eye. I knew what would happen if I did this so I dodged God for a few hours before I actually made the effort to do it. as I look back on that moment I realize how ridiculous it was to try and dodge an omnipresent being; but of course I thought I had it all figured out. So the time came when I finally had to face myself and for two reasons; one, God was not leaving me alone about it and two, I knew I wasn't going to find any peace until I did. So I went into the bathroom and looked up and saw my own face. I saw the freckles on my cheeks and the brown on my skin but God said to look up. Here it was the moment of truth, my own eyes. I looked up and made eye contact with myself and I froze.

This was a moment that changed my life, my path, and my course. I stopped and stared in my own eyes and felt such a fuzz all over me. I was no longer the freckles on my face or the brown on my skin, but I was Marisa. I was my past, my present, and my future. I was that little girl who wanted a father, that teenager who was suicidal for no real reason, that twenty something bartending for attention, that abused girlfriend and that rape victim. I saw the wounds of my iniquity and the scars of my pain. I saw the tears that God collected into the bags under my eyes and the stress of all the sleeplessness nights.

My skin crawled as I saw the sexual partners I gave my body to. My hearing left me as I heard all the negative things I have sowed into the world. I was locked onto my own eyes like my soul was gripping my throat like the deep frost of a late winter midnights snow. I saw who I was and I saw what I have become. I saw myself the way the world saw me; broken, battered, resentful, and imprisoned. I saw the woman at the well.

It was here that I was broken down; I was humbled in the midst of myself. I not only saw the core of my existence but I saw the darkness of my heart and the roots of my frown. It was here that I learned the valuable lesson of confession. I saw myself and had no choice but to admit that it was me and not some sick joke my mind was playing on me. My illusions of the perfect self that I created was no longer welcome here; I opened myself up to myself.

I began to mentally open the hands of my psyche and release the petals of the fragments of hell I held on to so tightly. The unforgiveness, the hatred, the bitterness, the self-loathing, the self-defeating, the mistakes, the disorder, the fire, the rain; the elements of sinful self. I ripped the band aids off of the wounds that I was nursing and allowed the sun of the father to touch them with his light. I looked up from the mud and cleared my eyes so that what I intentionally hid from myself was no longer a shameful secret. I faced it and it broke me even more. I began to sweat and gag on my own healing. I was being ripped to shreds from the inside out and there was nothing I could do about it; I was too far to quit but not far enough for it all to end, I was here in the midst of my deliverance.

It was during this time that I had to admit who I was and accept me. I had to confess my sin, my short comings, my fears, and my indiscretions and embrace the fact that I have fallen. I had to humble myself to my part and to my faults. I had to accept the fact that I could do much wrong and that I had done much wrong. It was a time to admit and commit, sit and forfeit, so I can die to survive. This was the beginning of the journey of the creation of the new creature that God said he will manifest once we submit ourselves to his will; this was the point where I had to separate the role of who affected me and the role of the "me" that has brought me to this point. As painful and as shameful this process was, it was life building essential and beneficial.

> *"It was a time to admit and commit, sit and forfeit, so I can die to survive."*

The "What": What truly happened vs. what you believe happened

The "what's" of our lives. These are the things that caused us to react in the ways that we have. The occurrences of our lives that cause us to go a certain way; we all have them. Some of us have been molested, raped, beaten, and lied to, abandoned, left behind, pushed ahead, set up, knocked down, saved, killed, depressed, oppressed, regressed, and degreased; many of us have been spiritually murdered and emotionally marked, physically judged and mentally manipulated.

These nouns of our lives have made us into the person we are today and many of us use these nouns as an excuse to behave in a manner that not only is displeasing to God but a burden to society. We go forth in our unforgiveness and anger and drink until we pass out in the streets. We get high and go out and cause a stir at the club; we protect our promiscuity with our child hoods and spread famine and disease of the organs and hearts. We go forth and allow the hatred of our pasts to cause us to yell in traffic, throw things at our spouses, and snap at our children.

These nouns are what control our daily thinking and operating and the sad part is that we have no control over them whatsoever.

In this section I wish to show how essential it is to confront the "what's" of our existence and be honest as to the consistency of those "what's". Let me first share Gods word;

1 Corinthians 2:6 – 11 NKJV

"⁶ However, we speak wisdom among those who are mature, yet not the wisdom of this age, nor of the rulers of this age, who are coming to nothing. ⁷ But we speak the wisdom of God in a mystery, the hidden *wisdom* which God ordained before the ages for our glory, ⁸ which none of the rulers of this age knew; for had they known, they would not have crucified the Lord of glory. ⁹ But as it is written: "Eye has not seen, nor ear heard, nor have entered into the heart of man the things which God has prepared for those who love Him." ¹⁰ But God has revealed *them* to us through His Spirit. For the Spirit searches all things, yes, and the deep things of God. ¹¹ For what man knows the things of a man accept the spirit of the man which is in him? Even so no one knows the things of God except the Spirit of God"

Now this scripture speak about the spiritual wisdom that is given to us through the power of the Holy Spirit which is a part of the triune of God; which makes its authority given directly from God being that the Holy Spirit IS God. I decided to include this section of scripture because it speaks about having the wisdom of God, the eyesight of God, and the hearing of God; the attributes of God. When God speaks of the hidden wisdom he speaks of the wisdom that he has set aside for the remnant. The wisdom that is hidden and ordained for those he has called. Inside of this wisdom God shows us the direct roots to the embodiments of our existence. The "nouns" of our existence, the "what's". In this hidden place God reveals what we are and the spiritual DNA that births the behaviors and words that we present each day. When we make the choice to yield to Gods will and his way, we are inviting him to bring us in this secret place. Although we may not know that we are in this place; but God says that he holds a special area for those who follow him and for those he has chosen for his specified purpose. In this place God does his greatest works; the works of the heart, mind, and soul. It's here that change is imminent and shifting is evident. It's here that we are broken and torn apart for the Lords sake so that we can be rebuilt with the fibers of the kingdom. Without the hidden wisdom of what we are, we cannot move forward into becoming "who" God orchestrates us to be.

Let me begin to examine the true "what's" as opposed to the disillusioned "what's". Let me give you an example, let's think back on one of our deepest and most influential relationships. We think back on that person we were loving on and remember how deep our emotions were embedded in that person, the time we invested, and the love that we felt. Like any relationship, there comes a point where things begin to sour; the spats become fights and the disagreements become battles. Everything they do gets on your nerves, everything they say is wrong, and everything they stand for becomes a direct sin…..in YOUR eyes. When the relationship finally break ups especially if it does badly, we begin to formulate the conclusion in our minds instead of examining what actually happened.

It's similar to what the enemy uses to pull us off track. The enemy will use alterations of reality to keep us in bondage. Here is where discernment and wisdom is so crucial because we must distinguish between what we think is happening and what is truly happening.

There was a moment in my life when I was so cast down and so burdened by what I thought was happening to me that the enemy had me convinced that taking my life was the ONLY remedy to my troubles. He distorted my image and made my hearing selective. I was drowning in a black cloud of death and by my own hand almost succumbed to the heaviness of my soul.

But God is faithful to those who seek after him; he comes for those whom he loves. I discovered that even when we cannot get ourselves up, God is willing and able to gird us up in his mighty arms. He bears our weight when our knees are weak and assists us forward when are feet our shuffling in place. He is faithful to his promise of being an ever-present help in times of trouble.

In my time of turmoil I felt as though I let everybody down, like I failed myself, my children, and at life; But God is faithful and close to the broken hearted. This was a point where I had no strength to move forward, but he was my body guard. He didn't say a word to me, he just scooped me up and carried me out of the shadow of death and into the path of life and resurrection. He didn't leave my side and didn't cast down my name even though the enemy had me to believe I was cast out of the kingdom. He had me convinced that I was the black sheep of life, but the reality was that he was trying to quench my purpose because he was threatened. What I saw in my natural was completely different than what was truly taking place in the spirit.

It was essential to me to be shown the differences of my existence. Before I was unable to tell the difference between what was true and what I was conjuring up in my own mind. The nouns of my being required confrontation. I was in a time where I had to confront what was brewing in my life. I had to stare it in the face or else it would have eaten me alive. It's in our delusions that death breeds because the falsehoods of our thoughts cause us to walk in a distorted sense of existence. In this distortion we perform, speak, and operate in a realm of inconsistency and uncertainty. God is the God of revelation and enlightenment; he opens our eyes to the truths of the spirit realm and the secrets of our purpose in him. He moves ahead of us and clears the uncertain path. He walks before us and lights the way we should go and gives us the truth of our iniquities; not to cast us down but to correct us so we may walk straight. In this season of battling my nouns, I discovered that God is favorable to us even if all we can do is lay down and look up.

The "Why": the acceptance of reality

The "whys" of our trials may be somewhat tricky to identify. There are some things in our lives that happen that we may never know why they happened. We sometimes question God and ourselves as to why certain things happened and when we don't receive the answers that we want, we become bitter and untrusting. There are many reasons why something can happen. In the story of Job, the devil went to God and snarled at the assumptions that there was no one on the earth that was faithful enough to him to withstand severe trial. He bragged about how world praises God in the good times, but once tragedy hits we are amongst the first out of his gates. The Lord rebutted and shown the light on Job as being faithful despite anything the devil could throw at him. God allowed Job to be tested but not killed and Job rose to the occasion. Although he didn't understand what he did to deserve such a shift in his fortune, he remained on the side of crying out to God instead of lying there and receiving death like his friends instructed him to do.

There are times when we may encounter testing to both strengthen and mold our character or to endure in the sight of the enemy to show him that we are amongst the called that God trusts with his gifts.

There are also instances when we are sent through the fire for the sake of somebody else's deliverance. There was a time when I was struggling with depression and suicide, abuse, homelessness, poverty, and fear. I received the Lord and savior as my redeemer and still wrestled with these things in abundance. As I grew and matured I began to look back as I was ministering to people and realized that a lot of the things that I endured were partly for the sake of those God had already ordained for me to encounter in my path. I have spoken to many suicidal individuals and found myself with such a care and compassion for their needs that seemed to be something that I didn't just learn from some training class; it was personal.

As I was delivered from the demon of suicide, I realized that the hell I experienced was shaping me for the hell that those around me are or will experience. I was being prepared for a mighty work and higher calling. Of course at the time I didn't want anything to do with this truth; but as I sit here on the other side of that hades, I realize that my pain had a purpose and my tears had a territory.

We ask God "why?" often because the pain may be unbearable, the stretching may be too much to handle, the fire may become too hot; but God instructs us to not become weary in well doing (2 Thessalonians 3:13) He unctioned us to endure the unpleasantness of our shaping because it is for our good and for his manifestation of his promises and prophecy. He promised us strength to endure and spoke the dominion within is to encounter and persevere through the wilderness of our preparation season. Moses wandered into the woods as a teenager when he was called to free the people of Israel, Jesus wandered into the wilderness to be tested when the prophecy was given of being the ultimate sacrifice. These two dynamic examples of preparation before purpose helps us to see that even though we are uncomfortable, we are still called what God said we are. Before the soldiers came for Jesus, he cried out to the father for the cup to be passed from him; but God had a purpose to fulfill.

As I was going through suicide attempt after suicide attempt, I cried out to God to just end my life so the turmoil and the pain would stop; but God had a purpose to fulfill through me and through my pain. He knew what I was enduring, but he strengthened my heart to not relent. Even in the shadow of death, I felt a pang in my heart that spoke a sweet, quiet voice that led my soul back towards the light of life. I took these examples and adopted them as the lifesaving skills I needed to walk through the valley of death and push through the swamp of my shaping.

Instead of being consumed as to why it was happening to me, I began to embrace the ideal of "why not me?" I had to look deep and look through the eyes of Christ to see how essential I was to kingdom. He exposed to me the hidden secrets of my purpose and I began to feel proud of my trials and celebrate my preparation. I adopted learning the way I did as a child in primary school; only difference was that this was for the kingdom of God, this was for my soul. I began to accept what was happening to me and going to God with my tears and fears instead of spending precious moments figuring out why it was me who had to suffer. The more I asked why, the more he showed me what I was causing myself, what he was allowing to happen, and what the enemy was trying to do. My "why's" became "okay's". It was here that I found the essential acceptance of my experience and laid down the questions and searched for meaning.

This was the season that I began to move forward in understanding the spirit realm and how God operated in every fiber of our lives. My desire to understand shifted from the moment to the essence; which allowed me to discover that with God, everything that happens is for the ultimate good of that which was prophesied at the dawn of time.

Romans 8:28

New King James Version (NKJV)

[28] And we know that all things work together for good to those who love God, to those who are the called according to *His* purpose.

Chapter IV
The Conceptuality of Letting Go: what needs to take place and how

What needs to take place?

Self-assessment – the first step is the self-assessment; the self-inventory of your emotions, your thoughts, your behaviors, and your upbringing. It's a list of the things that make you, you. While doing a self-assessment may be difficult at times, it is beneficial and essential. It allows you to search deep down and begin to pull on the things that make you who you are. Rising each day and assessing your feelings and then asking yourself where those emotions came from, will allow you to discern between demonic possession and personal lack of faith. Doing a self-assessment can catapult you into prayer; for example, if you wake up and you begin to feel heavy and suicidal you can assess that these feelings are coming from a demonic influence and begin to find the door of these manifestations. In contrast, if you wake up and you begin to smile uncontrollably you can go to God in prayer, praise and worship and exalt his Holy name.

A self-assessment will give you the key to the door that shows you who you are and how God sees you through his eyes. Assess yourself and your emotional, mental, and spiritual makeup so you can have a clear picture as to what you are bringing to God so he can do his perfect work with the whole you and not just the store front of you. Give the Holy Spirit the permission to get into your crack and crevices and be brave enough to explore those dark places as well. Have a clear idea of who you are so that the demon of disillusion cannot take deeper root into your mind and heart.

Self-honesty – I admit that being honest with myself was not something that is at the top of my list of things to do; but I have discovered that it is essential in every aspect of the word. Self-honesty is the beginning of deliverance; an addict doesn't realize they need help until they are honest about how bad their habit is; the same is with the comfort zone of pain. Until we realize how bad our baggage is affecting us, we will not be able to effectively let God into our hearts so he can pluck up the roots and peel off the petals of our damaged existence.

Denial is one of the greatest hindrances of our deliverance; when we think we do not have a problem, we will not take the steps to fix the problem. A man addicted to heroin will not walk into the Betty Ford clinic if he doesn't think that his heroin use is affecting his judgment to make sound, positive decisions. The hanging on to the roots of our iniquities will cloud the judgment of the mind to realize and embrace the fact that we are walking through our lives emotionally and spiritually dead.

The hardest part of admitting our issues to ourselves is the ideal that we are no longer as stable as we once thought. Going into our closets and admitting to ourselves that we are not as perfect as we would like the world to think; that we are not as together as we would like our families to think. Self – honesty is essential because it allows God to give us a true picture as to what we have become and what we are becoming. We give ourselves the ability to look into a mirror and see exactly what God sees, so we can surrender exactly what God already knows.

The spirit of grandeur and confusion lives within the disillusions of ourselves; but in self – honesty we are able to speak to ourselves honestly and go to God with exactly what we are struggling with so he can work perfectly. Now don't get me wrong, he doesn't need our help to do his work but without our admission to sin, we cannot speak to the demonic influence of it.

For instance, I set myself on a campaign to prove myself the opposite of crazy as every single ex-boyfriend spoke over me since the dawn of my existence. In this campaign I refused to acknowledge the roots and causes of my behaviors and mindsets. In my self-proclaimed denial, I was hindering my deliverance because the authority and power within me was not allowed to speak to the demons of instability, fear, confusion, anger, and unforgiveness. Once I was real with myself, I was able to come boldly and real to God. Even though he already knew what I was operating in, it was I who was blocking the work that God was wanting to do within me.

The devil was having a field day because he had me walking around in a field of grandeur when I was truly walking toe to toe with the legion of self-destruction. I didn't understand why I hated myself or wanted to die, but I did know that I had no idea who I was or why I existed; I was lost in my own self-denial.

Self – honesty saved my life, because it allowed me to see the spiritual DNA of my existence and operate in the true identity of the kingdom. Once I was honest with myself and faced the brokenness of my being, I was able to bring them to God and lay prostrate at the altar in all of my iniquities instead of just some.

Repentance and humility was something I began to live in while facing myself and embracing who I was became something that I invited instead of feared. I was able to look at myself in the natural and set realistic expectations for myself instead of beating myself up for not being the person that I never was in the first place. Self- honesty is the beginning of kingdom orchestrated deliverance and shaping.

Steps toward letting go:

- Physical
- Mental
- Emotional
- Spiritual

Physical – The first step towards letting go was with the physical. Physically I had to reassess my natural state. I had to find balance in my natural world. I had to review my diet and seek medical attention for those aches and pains that I ignored due to self-loathing. I had to face myself in the mirror and see who I was turning into. I looked at the bags under my eyes, I looked over my sleep habits, and my triggers. I did a full health assessment on myself and sought God on how to reverse the damage I have already done. I began to look to sleep as a purposeful event instead of something that happened after days of running on empty. I began to cut out the binges of fried foods and fast foods and fast to allow my body to naturally cleanse and extract toxins. I ate super foods and leafy greens so that my body could excrete fat and soak up a nutrient to replace the deficiency I endured for so long. I got my eyes checked and spent more time outdoors to fill my lungs with fresh air instead of the air of my bedroom and my self-pity. I made myself over by subjecting myself to Gods will and instruction for the body that he created in his image and in his timing.

Psalm 73:26New King James Version (NKJV)

[26] My flesh and my heart fail;
But God *is* the strength of my heart and my portion forever.

Mental- my mind was a battlefield of thoughts. I had seeds of doubt, fear, anger, confusion, and every other unrighteous element the enemy could muster up; but the Lord said that I should be renewed in my mind and lean not to my understanding. (Proverbs 3:5-6) It was a choice. My mind was under siege and for many many years I chose to live in the midst of that battle without even lifting my sword. I was overwhelmed in my thoughts and underestimated in the fight.

> *"I had to choose to cast down those thoughts of my past and replace them with the visions that God has given me."*

I had to make the choice to turn my mind over to Christ and to focus on the things of the Lord. Yes I had Gods word in my heart, but was it in my mind. I had to ask myself if my heart and my mind were on one accord. I had to choose to cast down those thoughts of my past and replace them with the visions that God has given me. It was a daily battle and an attentiveness to the things that popped into my head. When I thought about wanting to cuss someone out I had to be aware of what I was thinking and remember that I am a new creature and pull myself back. When my past began to creep up, I had to make the choice to recognize what was happening and what was coming, expose the cause/ root, and then make the choice to turn my back on that closed door and no longer try the knob to see if it's unlocked. I had to mental speak affirmations to myself concerning my power, my strength, and my position. I had to mentally remind my body to react in a slower mode and proceed with the caution of Christ.

I had to make the choice; it was up to me to tell my mind to line up to the word that was within my heart. It took a choice and a determination, from there God was able to cover me because I was able to recognize when to go to him with my trouble.

Ephesians 4:23

New King James Version (NKJV)

[23] and be renewed in the spirit of your mind,

Emotional – "you cannot be a whole being with a broken circuit" the emotions are the links between our physical existence and mental stability. It's our emotions that cause us to leap into healthy behaviors or nose dive into disastrous nonfunctional manifestations of over eating, negative speaking, and troublesome decisions. Our emotions make or break us, whether we want them to or not. It took me a good part of my life to understand the correlations between my emotions and my physical and spiritual being. When I was walking in my emotions I was operating in my emotions. I was causing myself death because I didn't "feel like" living or speaking life.

My feelings caused me to binge eat and attempt suicide. I was a walking time bomb simply because of how I felt. It was God who showed me 2 people dwelling within me; the emotional me and the real me. My emotions were flawed and it was that flaw that caused me to behave in a manner that was destructive to my very existence. Without God I would have allowed myself to go to hell simply because I didn't "feel like" I was worth more than the darkness I felt. My emotions led to the negative words that I spoke over myself and my children. My feelings ruled my decision making and caused me to settle for things that were well below Gods standard of existence for me. I was a victim of my own feelings. Those pesky verbs that got in the way of everything I did.

God revealed to me the inadequacies of the emotions that I relied upon to orchestrate my life. He showed me the deceitful heart and how without the holy spirits unction, I was destined to run into the same wall over and over again until I caused my own brain damage. I had to be saved, I had to be set free. I first had to recognize that my emotions were conditional. I first had to examine them as being the strings the enemy used to manifest his Marisa marionette. The only real life line the enemy had to my behavior and my destructive thinking.

Once I saw my feelings and emotions for what they were I was able to look to a different source for my joy. I never understood what joy was until I began to look to God and his characteristics for the source of my joy instead of how I was feeling that day.

1) I had to release the way I felt and remind myself that "despite of" was a true concept.
2) I had to go forth and tell my emotions that I was breaking up with them and that I was marrying the faithfulness of God's word.
3) I had to examine myself and repent and sever the line between my life and my feelings; for the sake of my life.
4) I had to make the choice to save my life by rearranging my life's influence. This was the point where I had to see my emotions as being separate from my conditional praise and seeing God as being the orchestrator of purposeful praise.

Spiritual - "Forgiveness is in the hearts of the righteous and the eyes of the diligent" he said. While we release these things to the Lord we are to release the embitterment and entanglement of resentment so that we may receive wholeness and cleanliness manifests through the Lord Jesus Christ. Although we may walk through the valley of our spiritual, emotional, and mental deaths, the Lord said that we shall fear no evil.

Letting go may be one of the hardest, most crippling things a person may ever do in their lives; saved or unsaved. We often convince ourselves that letting go is a sign of weakness or that the person who did us wrong does not deserve out forgiveness. We speak ourselves into bondage and begin to get uncomfortable with the thought of being free. We feel that if we let it go and heal, we are vulnerable to the world doing it to us again.

I was here; I was terrified of getting hurt again, terrified of feeling those feelings again and terrified of experiencing those tears once more. I was crippled in self-inflicted fear and degradation. I placed myself into complacency, I took the wheel back from God and in turn telling him that I no longer trusted his path or his guardianship of my heart. I felt that the best person to protect me was me. I shut myself down and laid myself down by the wayside. Instead of the quicksand consuming me, I jumped into it head first.

There came a point where the realization came that while I was protecting myself on my own terms, my wounds were not getting healed but just sitting stagnant and festering. Since I took the control out of God's hands, I never gave the wounds of my past and my present a chance to be cleaned and healed properly by the stripes of the son; instead I allowed the maggots of unforgiveness to feed off of my fear and decompose my faith.

The issue was I took it out of God's hands. I took back my trust and I internalized my struggle. God is gracious in all that he does. In my self-pity, he came for me and showed me who I was. He showed me the wounds of my past and the roots of my iniquity. He showed me the side of me that I was afraid to face. I had to look, I had to make up my mind and then I had to turn and look. Once I saw I began to realize that it was my absence from God that fueled my blood shed. It was time to release and be set free. I had to let it go and I had to place it down.

Laying down your guard is never easy; it opens the door to vulnerability, risk, fear, future hurts, and even death. But God reminds us that with him, through him there is no vulnerability and with him there is no fear. He promised to protect and to cover. When I discovered that it was time to release and allow God to pluck up, it was the hardest decision of my life. I knew what was coming for me and I knew what the process entailed. I knew full well that the road before me was risky, painful and sometimes embarrassing; but God said that it was worth it. I saw the enemy afar off and he was waiting patiently for the moment I took the first step so he could strike. I made my decision fully aware of what I was doing.

I was making the choice to live, to love, and to be set apart. I was making the decision to be cleaned out and healed. I was tired of bleeding and tired of walking in heaviness. I was sickened and weakened and I was tired of it.

I knew two things:

1) I knew that I was more than what I was going through,
2) I knew that I was far greater than what the enemy had said; so I had to go forth. I had to answer the call and I had to set upon the path towards God that I never knew was necessary.

My first task was forgiveness:

1) I had to embrace the ideal of forgiveness and not just read the word over and over again in the King James Version. It was time to live it instead of just read it. I was unctioned to go forth and walk in the concept that was foreign and painful to me. I remembered all the things that people did and how they didn't deserve the forgiveness that I was told to give; but then I was reminded of how I didn't deserve the forgiveness that I received. The devil would remind me of the tears that I cried and then the Lord would remind me of the

tears that he dried. I was literally on the edge of a cliff; looking down into the unknown abyss which was the Lords trust and faith and looking back to a dry, desolate land that I wandered with my unforgiveness and pain. I was faced with a choice and with a lifesaving decisions. I had to weigh the cost of my staying and the cost of my leaping.

2) I had to truly search myself and ask if I felt like dying from a broken heart or dying for a renewed mind.
3) I had to search the waters of my soul and gauge the cost of my life in pain or the blind walk of faith. I had to make a choice and God was not giving me more time to boil on it.

It was my time to leap or I would have been left behind. I found that I was more afraid of leaving God than I was of what could have been waiting for me at the bottom of this cliff once I leaped. Once I made the choice to leap out on faith, I began to feel a rush of every emotion and feeling a human being could ever endure. It was too late now, I had already leaped so now it was time to release. That's correct I had to release those things that I was holding onto for all those years, because the more I refused to the faster and harder I fell. It was time I looked myself in the eyes and made the choice to release the hurts I became so used to feeling, release the fears I became so used to resting in, the anxiety that I became complacent with. I had to face those wounds and turn my trust over to God to heal them. My heart pounded and my hands shook violently but I surrendered. I took a deep breath and watched my hands begin to unlock their grip on the bags stuffed full of years of resentment, bitterness, anger, frustration to family, friends, ex-boyfriends, strangers, myself.

My bones creaked as I loosened my grip, but the flakes of my unforgiveness began to chip away in the wind of my leap of faith. My layers began to shed as I fell into the abyss of the presence of God. In my release I found that the presence of the Lord was drawing near to my heart and in my steps towards forgiveness I found that the Lords eyes became brighter in my path. It was in my desire to be made whole and my attempts to forgive and release that I found the spiritual life that God promised to his children that seek after him and his word.

The spiritual wellness of my current position came from the act of releasing the pain that I held onto for the sake of complacency, the veto of the misguided concept of forgiveness that was planted into my mind by the enemy, and the inability to reopen the doors of my past once I release the key to the father's hands.

A Guide To Letting Go

The course of my life I have encountered many stages of grief but the one that always eluded me was the act of letting go. Without letting go, moving forward is difficult. When I was in my twenties I used to hang around a lot body building type of men. There was this one man who would train in water. They would strap up to 200lbs of weights to his arms and legs and he would run in the water; one lap up and one lap down. I watched him every week because I was impressed at the type of resistance that he was able to defeat each week he tried. Looking back on this, I remembered that the more weight the man put on, the slower he got during each lap. What this man used for exercise and muscle building, we often allow to defeat and define us. The more and more weight of our iniquities that we add to ourselves, the harder it will be to endure the resistance and limitations of our flesh. We may push through but our stride becomes slow and stagnant as the weight slows our momentum to the point of eventually standing still. As we progress and as God reveals, our spirits have the desire to want to go farther and to dig deeper; and while we may be able to endure a few strides, the fact remains that our movements will eventually stop. It took me years to realize that the reason that I was stagnant was because of the things that I was afraid to let go of. My comfort zone became the hell that my circumstances created and the unknown became the joy and peace of the Lord. Imagine a person afraid of letting go of pain. Imagine a person afraid to be happy; well that was me. It took me self-discovery and consecration to see that I was far more effective lighter than I was heavier and afraid. My movement was in my freedom. While resistance may be an exercise for the flesh, it is a death sentence to the spirit; and God always said that what is good for the flesh is death to the soul. The greatest lesson I learned was the practice of facing my iniquities and simply letting them go. Embracing the notion that God does not hold onto muck and mess, I had to realize that if I was to reflect the character of Christ, I would have to let go just as quickly as Christ. The death I was holding on to was digging my early grave and cancelling my anointing. A choice to be made and honestly, where I was the choice of life seemed much more enticing.

So I say to you my dear brothers and sisters, go to God and ask yourself exactly what are those things that creating the greatest resistance. Search for them and face them; then ask God to pluck them up while you release them from your grip. Hold your hands before you and make a fist. Imagine all the negative, decomposing, death riddled things that you have tried to hide and keep from your surface your entire life. All the excuses, the words, the wounds that have been causing you the maximum amount of resistance. Picture them, hear them, relive them for the last time; cry, sob, scream, and yell if you must. Once you have them within you're balled up fists, I urge you to open your fingers and watch those things fall to your feet and float away into the sky. Picture all those negative words, festering wounds, and self-destructive habits floating away and disappearing into the far off heavens of the father. As you open your hands, raise them to the sky and release the remnants of them to the father. Declare to yourself that it is out of your hands and that it is at the Lords feet. Feel yourself getting lighter and watch yourself in your spirit become straighter and taller, feel your back align and your head begin to rise. Declare and accept freedom as yours and begin to praise God for the chains that were broken and the path that was restarted. Begin to seek God and just love on him because your freedom is now. Declare that this is your independence day fore who the son sets free is free indeed and it is so. God loves you, you are free, and you are equipped to release, you just have to believe it in the Mighty name of Jesus. Amen.

Hebrews 2:4

New King James Version (NKJV)

[4] God also bearing witness both with signs and wonders, with various miracles, and gifts of the Holy Spirit, according to His own will?

My Reflection

In your reflection, take the time to be honest with yourself. Talk to yourself and begin to examine and face the things that you have been holding onto up until this point. Look into your reflection and crawl deep into your own eyes and stand firm in the face your giants.

Ask Yourself:

1. What am I holding onto?
2. What are my fears? And why?
3. What are my wounds?
4. What do I feel is standing in my way of giving my FULL self to Christ?
5. What is stopping me from moving forward?

Open Your Eyes:

1. Who does God say I am?
2. What does God say I am?
3. Why does God say I am?
4. Who are my thorns affecting?
5. How does my stubbornness affect my purpose?

Once you have looked into the eyes of the soul that has been carrying you your entire life; it's time to speak to that spiritual being. From here, begin to open the hands of your mind and visualize your fears, hurts, mistakes, and hindrances being transferred into the palms of the father. Visualize every giant that you have faced and watch them begin to fall, one by one, as God blows them over with his mighty breath. As you begin to release your thorns, use your voice to embrace the roses of Gods grace.

Speak Life:
1. Whom do I belong to?
2. Whose shadow do I dwell within?
3. How will being free benefit me?
4. Who relies on my strength daily?
5. What do I see when I look into my reflection?

Move Forward (I decree and I declare):
1. I am strong willed with strong faith
2. I am dynamically successful
3. I am free from the bondage of fear, hurt, shame, and self-loathing
4. I am bold in my speech
5. I am confident in who I am
6. I am a child of the living God
7. I am favored in all areas of my life

Prayer

Father in the name of Jesus I come to you on behalf of those who are hurting, those who are stuck, those are stagnant, those who are in bondage, those who are kept behind because of their inability to let go. Father I stand on Psalm 146:7 where you said that you give freedom to the prisoners. I stand on the promise that who the son sets free is free indeed in the name of Jesus. Lord I ask in accordance to Matthew 21:22 where you said that what we ask for in prayer we will receive. I ask that you speak to the hearts of those who are unable to let go, that you loosen their grip on their pasts and the offenses of their yesterday in the name of Jesus. That you release their minds from the thoughts of what was done in the name of Jesus, and that you release their spirits from the bondage of emotional wounds, disobedience, and ungodly soul ties. Father I come to you to ask that you heal the wounds of our pasts, that you rip off the Band-Aids of our present and allow the new skin of your righteousness to cleanse and cover the scars of our interactions in the name of Jesus. Father, I ask that you meet us where we are at and that you create in us a clean heart; a heart that is strong enough to face our iniquities, strong enough to face our fears, and strong enough to face our healing process. Lord we are seeking after your face, your power, your fire, and your mercy in this hour in the mighty name of Jesus. Lord you are the author, the healer, and the mender of our souls. You come in as a sweet covering to mend our broken lives and you stitch together the fibers of our beings. Lord I ask that you have mercy upon us and help us to let go of our grip on the things that are hindering and stunting us in the name of Jesus. Allow us to walk in healing and step out on faith so that we can be free to worship and honor you abundantly as you deserve. Lord I ask that you increase within us and give us the strength to turn to you and decrease. Lord speak to the very hearts of our beings and help us to battle the giants of our pasts. Lord come forth please in the name of Jesus and make us whole; pluck up the roots our iniquities and clean out the cobwebs of our minds. Lord shower your mercy down upon us so that we may dwell in your splendor. Have your way even right now in the name of Jesus so that we may be free.

Lord Jesus we decree and declare that the yokes of fear are broken in the name of Jesus. That the chains of confusion are broken, that the shackles of immaturity and lack of faith are shattered in Jesus name. I decree and I declare that every giant of darkness and broken spirits is defeated in our lives and the lives of our families in the name of Jesus. Lord we thank you for this prayer and we love you Lord as we are trusting you to mend these broken vessels in the only way that we know you can; and that's perfectly. Lord God touch your remnant and heal us so that we can move according to your will. We believe it to be done in the name of Jesus. We love you and we thank you, in the name of Jesus. AMEN

A Guide To Letting Go

I dedicate this book to my mighty sisters and brothers of Kingdom Keys ministry and to my devoted and beloved Spiritual parents Edward and Shonda Surratt and Racquel Stroud; thank you for your love, support, prayers, and encouragement. I love you All.

References

Soberplace: negative effects of unforgivness . (2009, December 24). Retrieved from soberplace.com: http://soberplace.com/negative-health-effects-of-unforgiveness/

websters. (2014, july). Retrieved from http://www.merriam-webster.com/dictionary/emotions

www.ingramcontent.com/pod-product-compliance
Lightning Source LLC
Chambersburg PA
CBHW020017050426
42450CB00005B/513